CLASSIC NFL GAMES
12 THRILLERS FROM NFL HISTORY

by Matt Scheff

12
STORY
LIBRARY

www.12StoryLibrary.com

12-Story Library is an imprint of Peterson Publishing Company and Press Room Editions.

Produced for 12-Story Library by Red Line Editorial

Photographs © Kathy Willens/AP Images, cover, 1, 27; AP Images, 4, 6, 7; Harry Cabluck/ AP Images, 9; Al Messerschmidt/AP Images, 11, 14, 17; Bettmann/Corbis, 13; Kevin Terrell/ AP Images, 18; John Gaps III/AP Images, 19; Reuters/Corbis, 21; Chris O'Meara/AP Images, 22, 28; John Bazemore/AP Images, 23; Marcio Sanchez/AP Images, 25, 29; David J. Phillip/ AP Images, 26

ISBN
978-1-63235-154-8 (hardcover)
978-1-63235-194-4 (paperback)
978-1-62143-246-3 (hosted ebook)

Library of Congress Control Number: 2015934299

Printed in the United States of America
Mankato, MN
June, 2015

Go beyond the book. Get free, up-to-date content on this topic at 12StoryLibrary.com.

TABLE OF CONTENTS

1

UNITAS LEADS THE CHARGE

The 1958 National Football League (NFL) Championship Game was between the Baltimore Colts and the New York Giants. It has been called "The Greatest Game Ever Played."

The star was 25-year-old Colts quarterback Johnny Unitas. Trailing 17–14 with just 1:56 to go, the Colts started a drive from their own 14-yard line. Unitas led Baltimore down the field with one long pass after the next. Three in a row went to star

Baltimore Colts fullback Alan Ameche runs into the end zone for the winning touchdown in the 1958 NFL Championship Game.

wide receiver Raymond Berry. With just seven seconds left, the Colts booted the game-tying field goal. The game was headed to overtime. It would be the first overtime game in the history of the NFL Championship.

It was sudden death. That meant the first team to score would win. The Giants won the coin toss. The Colts defense forced a quick punt. On came Unitas. The young star called all his team's plays. The result was an unforgettable 13-play, 80-yard drive. Fullback Alan Ameche finished it off. He blasted through the defense for a 1-yard, title-winning touchdown run.

Final score: Colts 23, Giants 17.

17
People, including players and coaches, in the game who are now in the Pro Football Hall of Fame.

- The score was close, but the Colts dominated. They outgained the Giants 460 yards to 266.
- Unitas completed 26 of 40 passes for 349 yards. He threw one touchdown and one interception.
- The game was played at Yankee Stadium in New York and was on national television.

THE GREATEST?

NFL fans love to debate which quarterback is the greatest in history. Was it Joe Montana? John Elway? Brett Favre? What about modern stars such as Peyton Manning and Tom Brady? Many old-school fans say it was Johnny Unitas. It's hard comparing quarterbacks who played in different eras. Passers today enjoy a lot more protection from officials. Defenders are limited by new rules. Players like Unitas never got to play under such passer-friendly rules. Yet he remains one of the most productive passers of all time.

COWBOYS AND PACKERS BATTLE IN "THE ICE BOWL"

Thirteen degrees below zero (-25°C). That was the temperature when the Green Bay Packers and Dallas Cowboys squared off on December 31, 1967. It was called the 1967 NFL Championship Game, but fans know it by another name: "The Ice Bowl."

It was brutally cold. Early on, defense ruled. Green Bay led 14–10. Then on the first play of the fourth quarter, Dallas ran a trick play. Running back Dan Reeves took the ball. Instead of running, he looked down the field. Reeves passed it to wide receiver Lance Rentzel for

Green Bay Packers quarterback Bart Starr prepares to take a snap in "The Ice Bowl."

a stunning 50-yard touchdown. The Cowboys went up 17–14.

With five minutes left, Green Bay got the ball at its own 32-yard line. Quarterback Bart Starr completed a series of passes to move his team into Dallas territory. Then running back Donny Anderson powered them to the 1-yard line.

Twice Anderson tried to punch it in. Twice Dallas stopped him. Starr called time out with just 16 seconds left. The Cowboys expected a pass play. A run would be dangerous. The clock could run out if it wasn't successful. Starr knew the Cowboys wouldn't be expecting it, so he called a risky run. He took the snap, followed his blockers, and lunged for the game-winning touchdown.

-48°

Wind chill, in Fahrenheit (-44°C), measured at kickoff of "The Ice Bowl."

- More than 50,000 fans watched the game on New Year's Eve at Lambeau Field in Green Bay.
- The Packers went on to defeat the American Football League champion Oakland Raiders in Super Bowl II.
- Several players were treated for frostbite. One fan died from exposure to the cold.

Steam rises from fans' breathing during "The Ice Bowl."

3

HARRIS HAULS IN AN "IMMACULATE RECEPTION"

Just what happened at Three Rivers Stadium in Pittsburgh on December 23, 1972? Pittsburgh Steelers fans and Oakland Raiders fans have two very different ideas. Yet nobody is really sure. The game they played that day may be steeped in more mystery than any other in NFL history.

The teams were locked in a defensive playoff battle. Both offenses struggled to move the ball. With 22 seconds left, Oakland clung to a 7–6 lead. Pittsburgh quarterback Terry Bradshaw took the snap from his own 40-yard line. Bradshaw fired a pass toward running back John Fuqua. As soon as the ball reached Fuqua, Oakland safety Jack Tatum slammed into him. The ball went flying backward. Steelers running back Franco Harris scooped it up just before it hit the turf. Then he ran it into the end zone.

Confusion reigned. A rule said that once Fuqua touched the pass, no other Steelers player could catch it. That is, unless a defender touched it first. Had Tatum touched the ball? He said no.

The officials huddled. They were uncertain. Officials didn't have instant replay back then. Referee Fred Swearingen even called the press box for help in making a ruling. Finally, they signaled touchdown. The stadium went wild over the Pittsburgh victory. And an NFL controversy was born.

Franco Harris of the Pittsburgh Steelers runs the "Immaculate Reception" in for a touchdown.

THINK ABOUT IT

Part of the reason this game was controversial was because TV cameras didn't capture it very well. How might things be different today, with dozens of high-definition cameras covering the action? In the end, how do you think controversy affected the game's popularity?

0

Total points scored in the first half of the game.

- The media dubbed Franco Harris's catch the "Immaculate Reception."
- Harris's 60-yard reception was by far the longest play of the day. Only two other plays went for more than 20 yards.

4

WINSLOW GUIDES CHARGERS TO EPIC VICTORY

It's a game called the "Epic in Miami." Yet at first, the January 1982 playoff game didn't look like much of a game at all. The San Diego Chargers jumped all over the hometown Dolphins. Behind quarterback Dan Fouts and tight end Kellen Winslow, they built a 24–0 lead by the end of the first quarter.

Miami coach Don Shula turned to backup quarterback Don Strock. It worked. Strock and the Dolphins charged back. They tied the game 24–24 early in the third quarter.

The score stood at 38–38 with three minutes to play. The Dolphins drove down to San Diego's 25-yard line. Then they went for the go-ahead field goal. Snap. Hold. Kick.

Winslow leaped in the air, just barely tipping the ball. No good! Overtime!

The overtime period stretched on. It was hot and humid. Players were exhausted, especially Winslow. He had been all over the field. Now, cramping, he struggled even to

79
Total points scored in the game, a playoff record at the time.

- Kellen Winslow caught 13 passes—a playoff record—for 166 yards and a touchdown.
- Dan Fouts completed 33 of his 53 passes for 433 yards. All were playoff records.
- Don Strock piled up 403 passing yards and four touchdowns despite not playing the first quarter.

move. Yet he battled on. Miami had another chance to win with a field goal. But again, it was blocked. Finally, more than 13 minutes into overtime, the Chargers ended the thriller with a 29-yard field goal.

San Diego Chargers teammates help Kellen Winslow (80) off the field after the "Epic in Miami."

MONTANA FINDS CLARK FOR "THE CATCH"

It was a clash between old and new. The Dallas Cowboys entered the 1981 National Football Conference (NFC) Championship Game as the conference's dominant team. The up-and-coming San Francisco 49ers were looking to take over that role.

It was a tight game. The Cowboys used a potent rushing attack, led by Tony Dorsett. Meanwhile, a young quarterback named Joe Montana led a powerful San Francisco passing attack.

The Cowboys led 27–21 with approximately five minutes to play. Montana and the 49ers took over deep in their own territory. The quarterback led his team 83 yards down the field to the Dallas 6-yard line. With less than a minute to play, the 49ers faced third-and-three.

Montana took the snap and rolled to his right. The Dallas rush was on. Montana spotted wide receiver Dwight Clark streaking across the end zone. Montana threw a high, lofting pass. Clark launched himself into the air and snatched the ball. Touchdown!

6'4"

Dwight Clark's height in feet and inches (1.93 m). He needed every inch to make "The Catch."

- San Francisco won despite turning the ball over six times in the game.
- The 49ers' win helped spark a new NFL dynasty.
- San Francisco went on to win four of the next nine Super Bowls.

THINK ABOUT IT

Joe Montana was known for staying calm under pressure. How do you think this helped Montana with the game on the line against the Cowboys? How might Montana's presence have affected his teammates?

Dwight Clark (87) leaps into the air to make "The Catch" in the 1981 NFC Championship Game.

With the extra point, San Francisco won 28–27. "The Catch" remains one of the most famous plays in NFL history. It helped make Montana one of the biggest stars in football.

ELWAY ENGINEERS "THE DRIVE"

The American Football Conference (AFC) Championship Game after the 1986 season was a classic back-and-forth battle. A week before, young quarterback John Elway had led the Denver Broncos to their first playoff victory in a decade. Now, he was trying to lead them to the Super Bowl.

The Cleveland Browns stood in his way. With the game tied 13–13 late in the fourth quarter, Browns

Denver Broncos quarterback John Elway drops back to pass during the AFC Championship Game.

quarterback Bernie Kosar struck. He rifled a 48-yard touchdown pass to put the Browns ahead. Denver's chances seemed dim after a muffed kickoff return. Elway took over at his own 2-yard line.

98

Yards gained by the Broncos on the final drive of regulation, earning it the nickname "The Drive."

- Rich Karlis's game-winning field goal was controversial. Many believe the kick actually hooked wide of the goal posts.
- This is the only AFC Championship Game ever to go to overtime.

What followed was one of the greatest drives in NFL history. Over 15 plays, Elway marched his team down the field. That included an amazing 20-yard pass when the Broncos faced third-and-18 near midfield. Elway capped off "The Drive" with a 5-yard scoring pass to Mark Jackson. Then Elway did it again in overtime. He led the Broncos 60 yards to set up the game-winning field goal.

THINK ABOUT IT

The quarterback is the most important player on a football team. If you ran an NFL team, what qualities would you look for in a quarterback? Do you value football skills or character more?

15

BILLS DO THE UNTHINKABLE

Houston Oilers 28, Buffalo Bills 3. The scoreboard at halftime of the January 1993 playoff game said it all. Dejected Buffalo fans watched as their team seemed headed toward defeat. Bills quarterback Jim Kelly was injured. Backup Frank Reich was struggling. Early in the second half, he threw an interception that Houston returned for a touchdown. That put the Oilers up 35–3. Fans streamed toward the exits.

Then something changed. Reich started whipping pinpoint passes all over the field. Just like that, the Bills were unstoppable. Before the third quarter was over, they'd scored four touchdowns. Then with just three minutes to go, Reich zipped a pass to wide receiver Andre Reed. Thirty-five straight points! It seemed impossible, but the Bills led by three.

The Oilers fought back. Quarterback Warren Moon led a frantic drive down the field. Kicker Al Del Greco capped it off with a field goal. That sent the game to overtime.

Houston won the coin toss. The Oilers started to march. Then Moon threw a costly interception. Buffalo took over deep in Houston territory. Two plays later, Bills kicker Steve Christie booted a 32-yard field goal. Comeback complete.

32

Points the Bills fell behind the Oilers in the third quarter.

- The Bills' comeback was the largest in NFL history.
- The Bills went on to the Super Bowl, where they lost to the Dallas Cowboys.
- The game is known in Buffalo simply as "The Comeback."

THINK ABOUT IT

Some say that building
on a huge lead is poor
sportsmanship. It's called
running up the score. The
Oilers led by 32. Yet they lost.
So should a team ever stop
trying to score? How big a lead
is enough?

DYSON FALLS A YARD SHORT

Super Bowl XXXIV in January 2000 was a clash of styles. The ground-and-pound Tennessee Titans were led by quarterback Steve McNair and running back Eddie George. The high-flying St. Louis Rams were the talk of the league. NFL Most Valuable Player (MVP) quarterback Kurt Warner led one of the most dynamic offenses in league history.

The Rams built a 16–0 second-half lead. But the Titans came back to tie it with just 2:12 to go. The Rams got the ball back.

St. Louis Rams wide receiver Isaac Bruce (80) races for a touchdown against the Tennessee Titans in Super Bowl XXXIV.

Titans wide receiver Kevin Dyson falls just short of a touchdown that would have won Super Bowl XXXIV.

On their first play, Warner tossed a pass to wide receiver Isaac Bruce. He darted 73 yards to the end zone. The Rams led 23–16.

But the Titans had one more chance. McNair guided them down the field. It was a race against the clock. With just six seconds left, the Titans were ten yards away. It all came down to one play.

McNair threw it to wide receiver Kevin Dyson over the middle. Dyson lunged toward the end zone. But Rams linebacker Mike Jones grabbed him by the leg. Dyson tried to stretch the ball over goal line, but Jones held firm. Dyson was down. The Titans were a yard short, and the Rams were the Super Bowl champs.

16
Points by which the Rams led in the third quarter.

- The Titans called their final offensive play "Silver Right." It was the first time they'd ever used it in a game.
- Mike Jones's big play is known simply as "The Tackle." ESPN.com rated it the second-greatest moment in Super Bowl history.

19

BRADY TUCKS IT AWAY

A New England snowstorm filled the air with flakes. The field was covered in white. The New England Patriots and Oakland Raiders battled through the weather in January 2002. The winner would earn a trip to the AFC Championship Game.

The offenses both struggled to move the ball in the snow. With less than two minutes to play, the Patriots trailed 13–10. They had the ball near midfield. Quarterback Tom Brady took the snap. The rush was on. Brady moved the ball as if to pass but then pulled it back. Suddenly, Oakland cornerback Charles Woodson slammed into Brady as his arm was moving. Brady went down and the ball came loose. Oakland recovered the fumble and started to celebrate.

The officials huddled. Then they made a call that shocked almost everyone. It wasn't a fumble. The little-known "tuck rule" stated that as long as Brady's arm had moved forward, as if to pass, the play was an incomplete pass instead of a fumble. It didn't matter that Brady had already tucked the ball back toward his body. The Raiders watched in disbelief.

312
Passing yards by first-year starter Tom Brady in the game. Of those, 238 came in the second half and overtime.

- The game helped spark a new NFL dynasty. The Patriots went on to win three out of the next four Super Bowls.
- The tuck rule was called one other time during the 2001 season. In that game, the call went against the Patriots.

The Oakland Raiders' Charles Woodson dives at New England Patriots quarterback Tom Brady in the controversial "Tuck Rule" play.

A few plays later, Patriots kicker Adam Vinatieri booted a 45-yard field goal through the blizzard to send the game to overtime. New England won the coin toss. Again, Brady marched them down the field. Another Vinatieri field goal ended one of the most shocking games in NFL history.

THE TUCK RULE

The infamous tuck rule was added to the rulebook in 1999. Few fans even knew about or understood it. That changed after the Patriots beat the Raiders. Fans and media alike bashed the rule. Finally, in 2013, the NFL agreed. It abolished the rule, allowing officials to decide the quarterback's intent with any forward motion of the ball.

BIG PLAYS RULE SUPER BOWL XLIII

The Super Bowl is the NFL's biggest stage. The game doesn't always live up to the hype. It certainly did on February 1, 2009, however. The Pittsburgh Steelers and Arizona Cardinals put on one of the most thrilling shows in Super Bowl history.

It was one big play after the next. Arizona trailed 10–7 with just seconds left in the first half. The Cardinals were at Pittsburgh's 1-yard line. Quarterback Kurt Warner dropped back and fired a pass. Linebacker James Harrison faked a blitz. Then he stepped back and intercepted Warner's pass in the end zone. Harrison was off to the races.

Pittsburgh Steelers wide receiver Santonio Holmes catches the game-winning touchdown in Super Bowl XLIII.

He rumbled down the sideline for a 100-yard touchdown. The Steelers took a 17–7 lead into halftime.

Then Warner and the Cardinals stormed back in the second half. Star wide receiver Larry Fitzgerald hauled in a 64-yard touchdown pass with just under three minutes left. Arizona now led 23–20.

It was Pittsburgh's turn to come back. Quarterback Ben Roethlisberger zipped passes all over the field. His favorite target was wide receiver Santonio Holmes. The two connected on a 40-yard pass to push the ball to Arizona's 6-yard line. With 42 seconds left, "Big Ben" took the snap. He looked left. He looked right. Finally, he heaved a pass into the back corner of the end zone. Holmes leaped up and grabbed it. Somehow, he managed to tap his toes in bounds before falling. Touchdown! The Steelers won.

131
Receiving yards by Santonio Holmes in the game. He was named Super Bowl MVP.

- The victory gave the Steelers their sixth Super Bowl title. That's the most in NFL history.
- Kurt Warner threw for 377 yards in a losing effort. That was the second most passing yards in Super Bowl history.

11

BROTHER FACES BROTHER ON THE BIG STAGE

Super Bowl XLVII in February 2013 featured a matchup unlike any other. The Baltimore Ravens and San Francisco 49ers were coached by brothers. John Harbaugh guided the Ravens while brother Jim Harbaugh led the 49ers.

Early on, it looked like a blowout for the Ravens. They led 21–6 at halftime. Then Baltimore's Jacoby Jones returned the second-half kickoff 108 yards for a touchdown. Now the Ravens led 28–6.

It seemed like lights-out for the 49ers. Then . . . the lights in the New Orleans Superdome really did go out. A 34-minute power outage brought the game to a halt. When the players finally returned to the field, it was like a switch had been flipped. Quarterback Colin Kaepernick led the 49ers on a frantic comeback. With 10 minutes to go, he scrambled

15 yards for a touchdown. That pulled San Francisco to within two points, 31–29. The 49ers went for a two-point conversion and the tie, but the attempt failed.

108

Yardage on Jacoby Jones's second-half kickoff return. It was the longest play in Super Bowl history.

- The final score was 34–31 for Baltimore.
- The Ravens took an intentional safety with just seconds left in the game. The play helped take valuable seconds off the clock.
- Joe Flacco was named Super Bowl MVP. He threw for 287 yards and three touchdowns.

24

Baltimore quarterback Joe Flacco led his team down the field, setting up a field goal. That gave the Ravens a five-point lead. The 49ers would need a touchdown. The crowd screamed as Kaepernick and the 49ers marched down the field. They reached Baltimore's 7-yard line. That's when the powerful Baltimore defense stepped up. The Ravens stopped the 49ers on four straight plays. A few plays later, it was all over. John Harbaugh and the Ravens were the champs.

Baltimore Ravens quarterback Joe Flacco celebrates after winning Super Bowl XLVII.

SEATTLE SUFFERS A STUNNER

Winning two Super Bowls in a row is rare. It had been done only eight times. Yet the Seattle Seahawks were on their way to making it nine. They led the New England Patriots 24–14 in the fourth quarter at Super Bowl XLIX in February 2015.

That's when Patriots quarterback Tom Brady went to work. He led the Patriots on two touchdown drives. The second gave them a 28–24 lead with 2:02 to go. But Seattle was not done yet.

The Seahawks got the ball back. They drove it to New England's 38-yard line. Quarterback Russell Wilson threw deep for wide receiver Jermaine Kearse. Kearse was falling

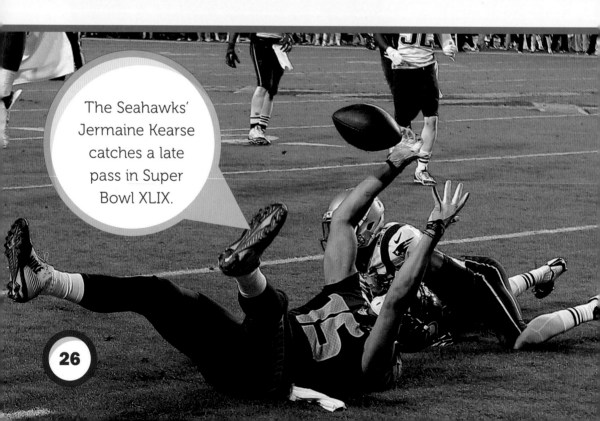

The Seahawks' Jermaine Kearse catches a late pass in Super Bowl XLIX.

The Patriots' Malcolm Butler makes the game-saving interception in Super Bowl XLIX.

as the ball got to him. He was able to tip the ball and keep it in the air. It was an amazing catch. Seattle was on the 5-yard line with about a minute left.

102
Marshawn Lynch's rushing yards in Super Bowl XLIX.

- Tom Brady was named Super Bowl MVP for the third time.
- Malcolm Butler had no interceptions and 22 total tackles all season before his famous play.

Running back Marshawn Lynch took the handoff next. He carried the ball for four yards. The Seahawks needed just one more yard to score. Lynch had played a great game. He was averaging more than four yards per carry. Most people thought the Seahawks would have Lynch run again. Instead, they passed.

Receiver Ricardo Lockette reached out to grab the pass at the goal line. Instead, Patriots rookie Malcolm Butler stepped up and grabbed it. Interception! Only 20 seconds remained. The Patriots ran out the clock to win their fourth Super Bowl.

FUN FACTS AND STORIES

- How cold was "The Ice Bowl?" It was so cold that the officials couldn't use their metal whistles. When one official tried, his lips stuck to the metal. Tearing them off left him with a bloody lip.

- The Houston Oilers were the Bills' victims in the largest comeback in NFL history. The team later moved to Tennessee and became the Titans. There, they got their revenge. On January 8, 2000, the Titans and Bills faced off in a playoff game. The Titans won it on a last-second kickoff return. Tight end Frank Wycheck threw a lateral pass across the field to Kevin Dyson. Dyson ran the "Music City Miracle" in for the game-winning touchdown.

- Check out the top three passing totals in Super Bowl history through the 2014 season. Notice anything in common?

  1) **Kurt Warner (St. Louis)**
     Super Bowl XXXIV
     414 yards
  2) **Kurt Warner (Arizona)**
     Super Bowl XLIII
     377 yards
  3) **Kurt Warner (St. Louis)**
     Super Bowl XXXVI
     365 yards

- Tom Brady and Charles Woodson, who forced the famous non-fumble in the "tuck rule" game, were college teammates at the University of Michigan. The two stars were still playing more than a decade later. In 2014, Woodson joked that Brady "owes me his house" because that play helped launch Brady to stardom.

GLOSSARY

blitz
A play in which a player who does not normally rush the quarterback does so.

controversy
A prolonged, often intense disagreement.

dominant
The most powerful.

draft
An event held each year in which NFL teams select players who are new to the league.

dynamic
Active and fast moving.

dynasty
A long-lasting period of dominance for a team or player.

infamous
Having a bad reputation.

lateral
A throw that travels sideways or backward.

press box
A section within a sports stadium usually reserved for reporters and league or team officials.

snap
When the center gives the ball to the quarterback to start a play.

sudden death
A format under which the first team to score wins the game.

wind chill
A measure of how cold air feels on the skin because of wind.

FOR MORE INFORMATION

Books

Doeden, Matt. *Football's Greatest Quarterbacks.* North Mankato, MN:
Capstone Press, 2012.

Frederick, Shane. *Side-by-Side Football Stars: Comparing Pro Football's
Greatest Players.* North Mankato, MN: Capstone Press, 2015.

Wilner, Barry. *The Super Bowl.* Minneapolis, MN: Abdo Publishing, 2013.

Websites

NFL Rush
www.nflrush.com

Pro Football Hall of Fame
www.profootballhof.com

Pro Football Reference
www.pro-football-reference.com

Sports Illustrated Kids
www.sikids.com

INDEX

About the Author

Matt Scheff is an artist and author living in Alaska. He enjoys mountain climbing, deep-sea fishing, and curling up with his two Siberian huskies to watch football.

READ MORE FROM 12-STORY LIBRARY

Every 12-Story Library book is available in many formats, including Amazon Kindle and Apple iBooks. For more information, visit your device's store or 12StoryLibrary.com.

WEATHER

Wind

by Ann Herriges

BELLWETHER MEDIA • MINNEAPOLIS, MN

Note to Librarians, Teachers, and Parents:

Blastoff! Readers are carefully developed by literacy experts and combine standards-based content with developmentally appropriate text.

Level 1 provides the most support through repetition of high-frequency words, light text, predictable sentence patterns, and strong visual support.

Level 2 offers early readers a bit more challenge through varied simple sentences, increased text load, and less repetition of high-frequency words.

Level 3 advances early-fluent readers toward fluency through increased text and concept load, less reliance on visuals, longer sentences, and more literary language.

Whichever book is right for your reader, Blastoff! Readers are the perfect books to build confidence and encourage a love of reading that will last a lifetime!

This edition first published in 2007 by Bellwether Media.

Library of Congress Cataloging-in-Publication Data
Herriges, Ann.
 Wind / by Ann Herriges.
     p. cm. – (Blastoff! readers) (Weather)
Summary: "Simple text and supportive images introduce beginning readers to the characteristics of wind. Intended for students in kindergarten through third grade."
 Includes bibliographical references and index.
 ISBN-10: 1-60014-026-2 (hardcover : alk. paper)
 ISBN-13: 978-1-60014-026-6 (hardcover : alk. paper
 1. Winds–Juvenile literature. 2. Weather–Juvenile literature. I. Title. II. Series.

QC931.4.H476 2007
 551.51'8–dc22   2006000617

Text copyright © 2007 by Bellwether Media.
Printed in the United States of America.

Table of Contents

Wind is moving **air**. It swirls around the earth.

Wind cannot be seen. But you can feel it touch your skin and pull at your clothes.

The sun helps make wind. **Sunshine** heats some parts of the land and sea more than others.

The air grows warmer above these heated areas. Warm air is light. It rises into the sky.

Cold air is heavy. It flows into spots where the warm air was. This movement of air makes the wind blow.

Sometimes the wind hardly moves. The air feels still. Smoke from a chimney rises straight into the air.

Sometimes the wind moves slowly. A **breeze** stirs the leaves on the trees and the hair on your head.

Sometimes the wind moves faster. It pushes sailboats across the water. It tosses kites in the sky.

The wind grows strong when a storm is coming. Dark **clouds** move across the sky.

The wind whips tree branches back and forth. It can turn your umbrella inside out.

Some storms can make **tornadoes**. These powerful winds twist from a cloud down to the ground.

Tornadoes can pull large trees out of the ground. They can lift cars and rip apart buildings.

15

Blizzards are snowstorms with strong, cold winds. It is hard to walk into the wind in a blizzard.

The wind can blow snow
into giant **drifts**.

Hurricanes are huge storms that form over the ocean. They have powerful winds.

eye

Hurricanes are shaped like doughnuts. Winds spin around a hole in the middle called an **eye**.

Hurricanes hit land with great force. The wind pushes tall waves on shore. It can blow down trees and buildings.

A strong wind can turn back into a gentle breeze. The wind is always changing. It carries weather around the earth.

Glossary

air—a mixture of gases around the earth that cannot be seen

blizzard—a snowstorm with strong winds, heavy snow, and cold temperatures

breeze—a gentle wind

cloud—tiny drops of water or crystals of ice that float together in the air

drift—a pile of snow made by the wind

eye—the calm, clear center of a hurricane

hurricane—a powerful, spinning storm with very strong winds; hurricanes form over the Atlantic Ocean and the Caribbean Sea.

sunshine—light from the sun

tornado—a fast-moving, whirling wind that touches the ground; a tornado looks like a dark, cone-shaped cloud.

To Learn More

AT THE LIBRARY
Bauer, Marion Dane. *Wind*. New York: Aladdin, 2003.

Cobb, Vicki. *I Face the Wind*. New York: HarperCollins, 2003.

Gibbons, Gail. *Weather Words and What They Mean*. New York: Holiday House, 1990.

Karas, G. Brian. *The Windy Day*. New York: Simon & Schuster, 1998.

ON THE WEB
Learning more about the weather is as easy as 1, 2, 3.

1. Go to www.factsurfer.com

2. Enter "weather" into search box.

3. Click the "Surf" button and you will see a list of related web sites.

With factsurfer.com, finding more information is just a click away.

Index

The photographs in this book are reproduced through the courtesy of: Laurie Stracan/Alamy, front cover; NPA/Getty Images, p. 4; Gloria-Leigh Logan, p. 5; Angelo Cavalli/Getty Images, pp. 6, 18-19; Michael Busselle/Getty Images, p. 7; Jim Cummins/Getty Images, p. 8; Jean-Marc Truchet, p. 9; Simone van den Berg, p. 10; stevegeer, p. 11; maodesign, p. 11(inset); Chris Windsor/Getty Images, pp. 12-13; Carsten Peter/Getty Images, pp. 14-15; altrendo nature/Getty Images, p. 16; Comstock Royalty Free, p. 17; Juan Martinez, p. 19; Ken Briggs/Getty Images, p. 20; Martin Barraud, p. 21.